ZEN
~ as ~
# F*CK

for You & Me

A JOURNAL FOR DITCHING THE SMALL STUFF
AND LOVING THE SH*T OUT OF YOUR RELATIONSHIP

Monica Sweeney

CASTLE POINT BOOKS
NEW YORK

THIS BOOK BELONGS TO:

_____

_____

GET READY *for the*
SWEET STUFF!

Embrace those happy tingles, be each other's biggest fucking fans, and find ways to agree and disagree with more tranquility. In the pages to come, you and your partner will *definitely not get into an argument about whose turn it is to fill out this journal,* but instead wander hand-in-hand through exercises that allow you to show one another love, appreciate each other for the little things, and ditch the shit that doesn't matter.

Whether you are as clear in your path as copilots, as supportive as teammates, as in sync as Bert and Ernie, or as lovingly dysfunctional as characters in a rom-com, there are all sorts of ways to let your love be fucking spectacular. Nobody likes sleeping on the fucking couch, so be humble and sincere with your responses! Express your love like you really fucking mean it, turn challenges into opportunities to get closer, and find ways to stay super-smitten.

Snuggle up and get sensitive as fuck with your love!

"I just want to be friends.
Plus a little extra.
Also, I love you."

—DWIGHT SCHRUTE, *THE OFFICE*

You're my FUCKING FAVORITE

Some people like to scatter rose petals all over the floor to express their love. That's cool! But so is scattering *compliments*. Let your words of affirmation flutter down onto each of the categories below. (And, no one has to clean up a rose-petal graveyard after!)

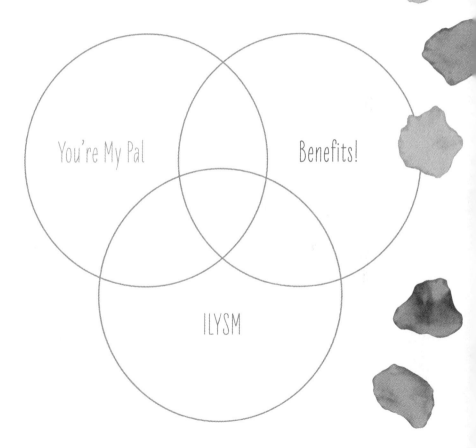

You're My Pal

Benefits!

ILYSM

"He told me he doesn't want my help, so I'm just going to play the supportive partner and watch him fail."

—DAVID ROSE, *SCHITT'S CREEK*

FAILURE: A NATURAL APHRODISIAC

Nothing stokes the fires of love like someone crashing and burning! While communication and support in a relationship are genuinely important, sometimes you just have to suppress that *I'm just trying to help!* instinct and let shit happen. When was a time when you could have taken a step back, held your opinion, or a moment when a minor fiasco turned funny?

You:

_____

_____

_____

_____

_____

Me:

_____

_____

_____

_____

_____

_____

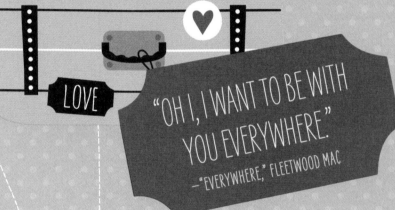

"OH I, I WANT TO BE WITH YOU EVERYWHERE."
— "EVERYWHERE," FLEETWOOD MAC

STICK *with* ME, KID

Well, maybe not *all* the time. (Autonomy is important!) But knowing you want to be almost-everywhere, almost-all-the-time with the same person is a pretty fucking spectacular feeling. Where were you when you first had that feeling? Where do you want to go with each other next?

You:

_____

_____

_____

_____

_____

_____

Me:

_____

_____

_____

_____

_____

_____

"*Listen, my body is attracted*
TO YOUR BODY,
but when you speak it makes
MY BRAIN ANGRY."

—MINDY KALING

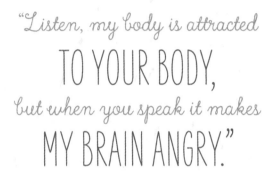

YOU'RE SO CUTE
When You're Mad

Not everyone communicates the same way when they're about to blow their fucking lid—some stew in silence, others say things they want to take back, and some people ball up their fists and stomp their feet like adorable giant babies. What's the best thing your partner can do to help you quell your frustrations when you are about to lose your shit?

You:

Me:

I LIKE LIKE YOU

It's not every day you find someone who thinks your personality quirks, mannerisms, or intensity about obscure topics that no one else cares about is fucking rad. What are some of the little things you like about each other?

You:

_____

_____

_____

_____

_____

_____

Me:

_____

_____

_____

_____

_____

_____

_____

MUTE ME, MAYBE

Some statements are worth confronting, like hurtful comments or cold-blooded threats to eat your leftovers. But other verbal faux pas can be left alone, like unsolicited opinions or deeply irrational ideology about whether pineapple is okay on pizza. What is the funniest topic upon which you have disagreed? What positive thoughts will allow you to rise above a comment you don't like?

You:

_____

_____

_____

_____

_____

_____

Me:

_____

_____

_____

_____

_____

_____

"My heart's in the right place. I know, 'cause I hid it there."

—CARRIE FISHER

SWING and a MISS

Accidentally fucking up sure is terrifying! When have you tried to do right by your partner but didn't convey it the way you wanted to? How would you show what was in your heart or try again if given the opportunity?

You:

_____

_____

_____

_____

_____

_____

_____

Me:

_____

_____

_____

_____

_____

_____

_____

"I CAN'T BELIEVE I
CAPTURED YOUR HEART."

—"WAKE ME," BLEACHERS

LIGHT of My LIFE

Maybe for you, finding love was a gentle process of capturing just the right firefly in your jar to light up your world, or maybe you kept swatting at lots of bright lights and burned the shit out of yourself in the process. What amazes you about your partner? What makes you feel excited that they chose you?

You:

_____

_____

_____

_____

_____

_____

Me:

_____

_____

_____

_____

_____

_____

_____

"THAT'S WHEN YOU KNOW YOU'VE FOUND SOMEBODY SPECIAL. WHEN YOU CAN JUST SHUT THE FUCK UP FOR A MINUTE AND COMFORTABLY ENJOY THE SILENCE."

—MIA WALLACE, *PULP FICTION*

QUIET, *Please*

Put sixty seconds on the clock. STFU and look into your partner's eyes while the moments tick by. Is your instinct to laugh, look away, tear up, make out? Describe what felt good or what felt uncomfortable in this minute of silence together.

You:

_____

_____

_____

_____

_____

_____

Me:

_____

_____

_____

_____

_____

_____

"How was I to know you were in peril? You keep everything inside, like a bashful clam!"

—MOIRA ROSE, SCHITT'S CREEK

Shucking AMAZING!

Open up that hard shell and get to the good stuff. Whether it's something deep and vulnerable to you or just making a fucking decision about where to eat, in what ways would it be better for both of you to share how you are feeling?

You:

_____

_____

_____

_____

_____

_____

_____

Me:

_____

_____

_____

_____

_____

_____

"Never Sent. Never Signed."

—ABRAHAM LINCOLN

THE ART of the "HOT LETTER"

Steamy storytelling is one brand of hot writing, but this hot letter is all about cooling your jets. When you are feeling upset and compelled to say or write words that might be hurtful, consider writing out a draft of your frustrations, waiting until you have calmed down, and then deleting it or rewriting it to be more measured and loving. Write something sweet or sexy here that you *would* like to send and sign to one another.

You:

_____

_____

_____

_____

_____

Me:

_____

_____

_____

_____

_____

_____

BUT, REALLY.

Say it like you mean it. People can spend a whole lot of time throwing *I love yous* around like fucking confetti or withholding them because they worry confetti is messy and maybe a little scary. When it comes down to it, though, confetti is extremely effective at its job. Sprinkle each other with some earnest *I love yous* here, or describe what saying it means to you.

You:

_____

_____

_____

_____

_____

_____

Me:

_____

_____

_____

_____

_____

_____

STATE of the UNION

Give your relationship a commanding address. Whether you prepare boisterous speeches in support of one another or sit down to make a list of goals, consider what you'd like to see, do, or achieve in the next months or year of your union. What are the most important points on your agenda? What shit do you need to vote out?

You:

_____

_____

_____

_____

_____

_____

_____

_____

_____

_____

_____

_____

_____

Me:

♥

"Don't try to participate IN ANYONE ELSE'S IDEA of what is SUPPOSED TO HAPPEN in a relationship. YOU WILL FAIL."

—*SCRAPPY LITTLE NOBODY*, ANNA KENDRICK

SUCCESS!

There are no rules here. Your relationship does not have to have a particular track, a set of milestones, or a normal code of conduct (outside of the basics like actually enjoying each other's company). What are the ways your relationship is a little different from what people expect? What about that do you fucking love?

You:

_____

_____

_____

_____

_____

Me:

_____

_____

_____

_____

_____

"MY LOVE FOR YOU HAS NO
STRINGS ATTACHED.
I LOVE YOU FOR FREE."

—STILL LIFE WITH WOODPECKER, TOM ROBBINS

YOUR MONEY'S No GOOD HERE

Keeping an emotional tab of what you owe one another in small favors, gestures, or visits with the in-laws is a really cute way to get into a giant argument! Cut that shit out. What about loving each other is free and easy? What feels so good it makes your heart feel rich?

You:

_____

_____

_____

_____

_____

Me:

_____

_____

_____

_____

_____

_____

"OBVIOUSLY, IF I WAS SERIOUS ABOUT HAVING A RELATIONSHIP WITH SOMEONE LONG-TERM, THE LAST PEOPLE I WOULD INTRODUCE HIM TO WOULD BE MY FAMILY."

—*ARE YOU THERE, VODKA? IT'S ME, CHELSEA*, CHELSEA HANDLER

FAMILY MATTERS

Look at all those skeletons in the closet – how fun! Families have all sorts of funky, funny, or slightly terrifying dynamics. How does your partner handle your family weirdness in a way that makes you feel happy or relieved?

You:

_____

_____

_____

_____

_____

_____

Me:

_____

_____

_____

_____

_____

_____

IS This ANNOYING?

It's good to have self-awareness of the things that make you unique in your relationship. In what ways do you think you might be difficult that your partner seems to adore or tolerate with a ton of fucking grace?

You:

_____

_____

_____

_____

_____

_____

Me:

_____

_____

_____

_____

_____

_____

_____

"For you, a thousand times over."

— *THE KITE RUNNER*, KHALED HOSSEINI

ALWAYS and FOREVER-ISH

Promises of eternity and to committing thousands of hours of your life to a partner can be—intimidating? Exciting? Fucking petrifying? Consider the ways your partner makes you feel jazzed up about continually moving forward together. Big act or small, what could you do a thousand times over for their benefit?

You:

_____

_____

_____

_____

_____

_____

Me:

_____

_____

_____

_____

_____

Charlie Brown:

I THOUGHT BEING IN
LOVE WAS SUPPOSED TO
MAKE YOU HAPPY.

Linus van Pelt:

WHERE'D YOU
GET THAT IDEA?

— *PEANUTS*

HAPPY TIDINGS

Being in love is exhilarating, and it can bring unbelievable tidal waves of happiness. When the tides calm, though, you still need to know how to swim, float in the sunshine, or cling—white-knuckled—to that surfboard on your own. What are the things that bring you happiness outside of that excitement with your partner, or that they can support by giving you more room to paddle?

You:

_____

_____

_____

_____

_____

Me:

_____

_____

_____

_____

_____

_____

Good Listeners
MAKE GREAT LOVERS

Who's up for a game of risk? Write down the name of the person who you think is always right. (Just kidding.) How could you be a better listener to your partner? If you are passionate about something upon which you have disagreed in the past, what can your partner do to hear you out?

You:

_____

_____

_____

_____

_____

Me:

_____

_____

_____

_____

_____

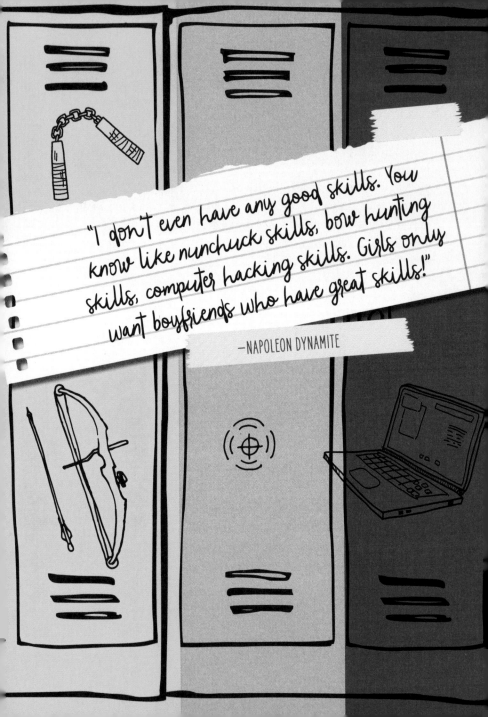

"I don't even have any good skills. You know like nunchuck skills, bow hunting skills, computer hacking skills. Girls only want boyfriends who have great skills!"

—NAPOLEON DYNAMITE

IMPRESSIVE!

Oh my! Such talent, such grace—you are just so great. Whether you are a real natural at incredible feats like scaling the highest mountain, speaking multiple languages, or you just make a fucking killer PB & J, those skills come in handy when sending pheromones your partner's way. What skills do *they* possess that get you all starry-eyed or that first drew you in?

You:

_____

_____

_____

_____

_____

Me:

_____

_____

_____

_____

_____

_____

"I LET IT HANG
OUT AND HOPE
MY PERSONALITY
WILL SUFFICE."

—NAOMI EKPERIGIN,
2 DOPE QUEENS

I ONLY HAVE *Eyes for You*

The good thing and the bad thing about long-term relationships is that couples get comfortable. Too comfortable? Maybe! But the beautiful thing about getting to know someone is you can drop the fucking pageantry of trying to look perfect all the time. What do you appreciate most about being relaxed around your partner? In what ways do they make you feel attractive even when you feel a little *bleh*?

You:

_____

_____

_____

_____

_____

Me:

_____

_____

_____

_____

_____

"REAL LIFE IS LIKE A CONSTANT YELP REVIEW, EVERYONE HAS NOTES ON HOW THE EXPERIENCE COULD BE IMPROVED."

—*I MIGHT REGRET THIS*, ABBI JACOBSON

FIVE STARS!

Funny how nitpicking the shit out of each other doesn't lead to romance. Write some positive reviews here. What makes you excited to keep coming back?

You:

_____

_____

_____

_____

_____

_____

_____

Me:

_____

_____

_____

_____

_____

_____

_____

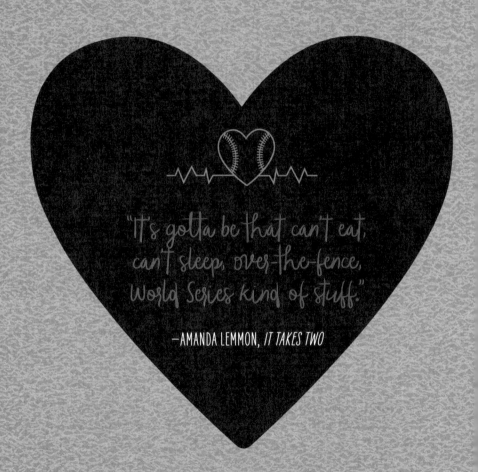

"It's gotta be that can't eat, can't sleep, over-the-fence, World Series kind of stuff."

—AMANDA LEMMON, *IT TAKES TWO*

THAT Good SHIT!

Every relationship goes through its droughts, disappointments, or even curses—but there are moments when you know you've hit it out of the fucking park. Replay a memory when you realized you found that good, good kind of love.

You:

_____

_____

_____

_____

_____

_____

_____

Me:

_____

_____

_____

_____

_____

_____

_____

"A PSYCHIC RECENTLY LOOKED RIGHT INTO THE ETERNAL COSMOS AND THEN RETURNED TO ME WITH THIS ELEGANT YET CRYPTIC MESSAGE: *GROW UP*."

—*LITTLE WEIRDS*, JENNY SLATE

GET It TOGETHER!

Some ghosts from childhood past are great, like candy necklaces, knowing the lyrics to every animated film ever made, or the adrenaline rush unique to playing *Hungry Hungry Hippos*. But adult things, like equitable distribution of housework, raising living beings, or filing your taxes, are really effing important. In what areas would you like your partner to take on more responsibility?

You:

_____

_____

_____

_____

_____

Me:

_____

_____

_____

_____

_____

_____

"It's enough for me to be sure that you and I exist at this moment."

—*ONE HUNDRED YEARS OF SOLITUDE*, GABRIEL GARCÍA MÁRQUEZ

PRESS Pause ⏸

What are you sure of right now? What about your relationship is as cozy as a damn blanket?

You:

_____

_____

_____

_____

_____

_____

_____

Me:

_____

_____

_____

_____

_____

_____

HEY, JEALOUSY!

Jealousy, you awful creature! Moments of jealousy occur on a sliding scale of totally justified to thunderous clouds of nonsense conjured from thin air. What about the experience of jealousy do you find most difficult?

You:

_____

_____

_____

_____

_____

_____

_____

_____

_____

_____

_____

Me:

"Time is how you spend your love."

—*ON BEAUTY*, ZADIE SMITH

LOVE YOU *for* E.T.E.R.N.I.T.Y

Expressing your love isn't about racking up anniversaries or putting in long-ass hours to prove your dedication, necessarily. But showing up for your partner for the big and small stuff, making good use of your time together, or even knowing when you both need to GTFO of each other's way are all expressions of devotion. What kind of time do you want together? When has your partner's respect for your time together made you feel loved?

You:

_____

_____

_____

_____

_____

Me:

_____

_____

_____

_____

_____

"My precious!"

—GOLLUM, *THE RETURN OF THE KING*

BE MINE

Wanting your partner all to yourself because they are just so shiny and pretty is natural. Actively insisting on it is *a bit much*. When do you most need to step back so each of you can share your sparkle with others? What about having independent space outside of your relationship improves it?

You:

_____

_____

_____

_____

_____

Me:

_____

_____

_____

_____

_____

_____

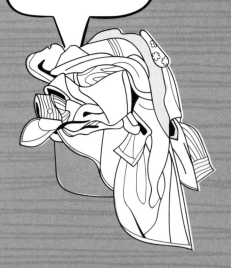

DIY PERFECTION

Make a list of the imperfections that make your relationship stronger, sillier, or that make your dynamic unique. What about these flaws are fucking great, or alternatively, worth working on? What about them make you more resilient with each other?

You:

_____

_____

_____

_____

_____

_____

Me:

_____

_____

_____

_____

_____

_____

_____

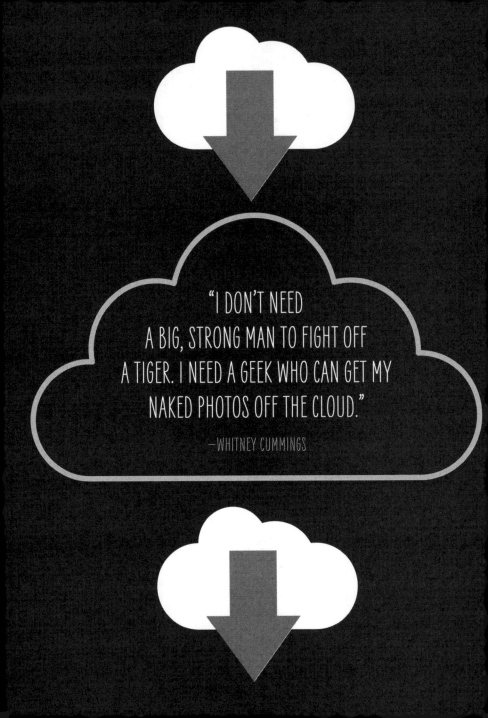

"I DON'T NEED
A BIG, STRONG MAN TO FIGHT OFF
A TIGER. I NEED A GEEK WHO CAN GET MY
NAKED PHOTOS OFF THE CLOUD."

—WHITNEY CUMMINGS

So NEEDY!

Everyone has needs, and some of them will surprise you. What are your needs? How do you fulfill each other's needs in positive ways?

You:

_____

_____

_____

_____

_____

_____

_____

Me:

_____

_____

_____

_____

_____

_____

"THANK YOU, NEXT

—"THANK YOU, NEXT," ARIANA GRANDE

LOVE for the EXES

Hold on, stay with me! Think of the elements of your past relationships that made you into a better partner, that built positive esteem, or that taught you lessons that help you now. In what ways has your past brought you two together?

You:

_____

_____

_____

_____

_____

Me:

_____

_____

_____

_____

_____

_____

"I just want to
BE SOMEBODY
to someone—
SOMEONE TO YOU."

—"SOMEONE TO YOU," BANNERS

YOU are My SOMEBODY!

What does your partner do that brings you a ton of fucking pride?
What kind of pride do you hope they have in you?

You:

_____

_____

_____

_____

_____

_____

Me:

_____

_____

_____

_____

_____

_____

LOADING . . .

"Before you marry a person,
you should first make
them use a computer with
slow Internet service to see
who they really are."

—WILL FERRELL

SHORT FUSES!

One of you has the shorter fuse—who is it? Is the other person holding the lighter or the fire extinguisher as a result?

You:

_____

_____

_____

_____

_____

_____

Me:

_____

_____

_____

_____

_____

_____

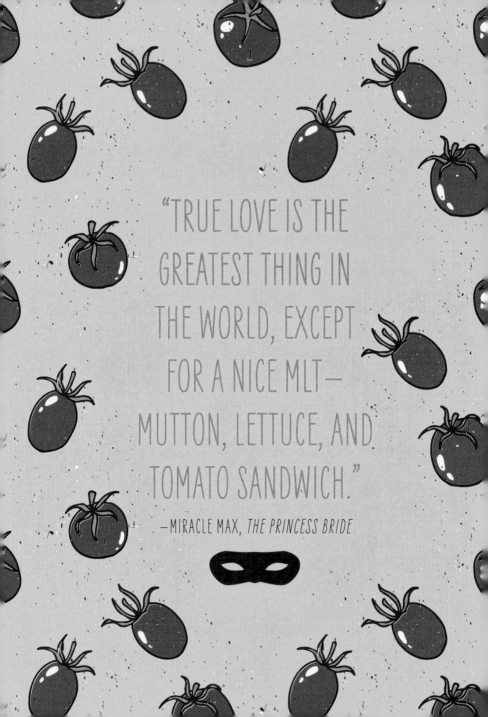

"TRUE LOVE IS THE GREATEST THING IN THE WORLD, EXCEPT FOR A NICE MLT— MUTTON, LETTUCE, AND TOMATO SANDWICH."

—MIRACLE MAX, *THE PRINCESS BRIDE*

I LOVE *you* MORE THAN!

You:

I love you more than _____!

Me:

I love you more than _____!

VIDEO GAMES

SNACKS   TV

PIZZA   FANTASY

DOUGHNUTS

PUPPIES   MY DUMB HOBBY

BEYONCÉ

SPORTS

EVERYONE ELSE   WIFI

SEX   ICE CREAM

BOOKS

WORK

COOKIES

"To forgive is an act of compassion...It's not done because people deserve it. It's done because they need it."

—RUPERT GILES, *BUFFY THE VAMPIRE SLAYER*

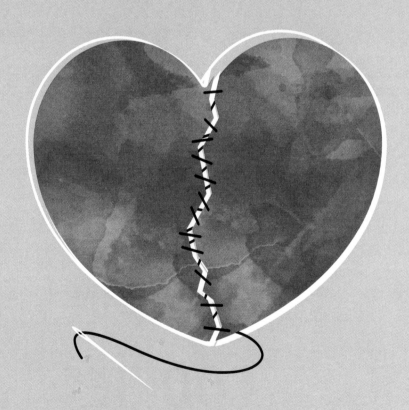

FORK Over FORGIVENESS

Be generous with your compassion. Start with something small, like forgiving one another for hogging the sheets or eating the last cookie like a fucking *monster*. What other elements of forgiveness would lead to progress in your relationship?

You:

_____

_____

_____

_____

_____

_____

Me:

_____

_____

_____

_____

_____

_____

_____

_____

WRONG-O

It's a short walk off that cliff when you find yourself ready to say something you can't take back. What calming methods can you pursue when your frustrations are running high? Whether it's taking a deep breath and quietly singing, "Don't be an asshole!" to yourself, finding a distraction, or yelling into a pillow, find ways to filter out your frustrations before they do damage.

You:

_____

_____

_____

_____

_____

Me:

_____

_____

_____

_____

_____

_____

YOU are My STAR!
(BUT ALSO, PRIORITIES...)

Write what's most important to you in the stars below. How are your focal points in life similar? If they aren't even in the same fucking galaxy, what compromises should you make?

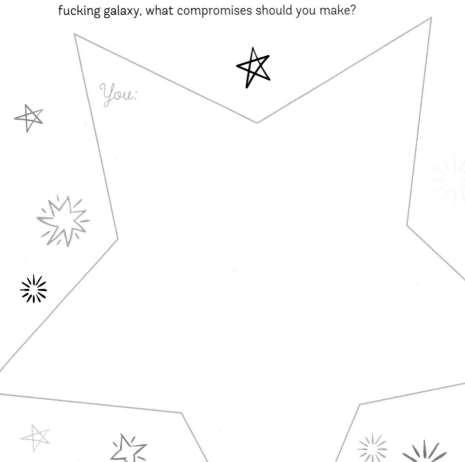

You:

Me:

"Yeah, he's
FUCKING CRAZY
but he's still my baby."

—"BABY," BISHOP BRIGGS

♥

LOVE YOU Like CRAZY

What are the things your partner does with intensity that you think are weird, wild, or downright batshit? Do you want this behavior to tone down or up?

You:

_____

_____

_____

_____

_____

_____

Me:

_____

_____

_____

_____

_____

_____

_____

KEEP *It* CLASSY!

Or not. Make it elegant or get down with whatever weird shit you're into. Describe the perfect date night.

You:

_____

_____

_____

_____

_____

_____

_____

_____

_____

_____

_____

_____

_____

_____

_____

_____

_____

_____

Me:
_____
_____
_____
_____
_____
_____
_____
_____
_____
_____
_____
_____
_____
_____
_____
_____
_____
_____
_____
_____
_____
_____

"DO YOU WANT ME TO TELL YOU SOMETHING REALLY SUBVERSIVE? LOVE IS EVERYTHING IT'S CRACKED UP TO BE."

—*FEAR OF FLYING*, ERICA JONG

SUCKERED IN

That good old rom-com formula exists for a reason. Describe the ways your partner meets or exceeds your expectations about love and the ways your relationship differs from what you had in mind.

You:

_____

_____

_____

_____

_____

_____

_____

Me:

_____

_____

_____

_____

_____

_____

_____

_____

"GUYS LOVE IT WHEN YOU CAN SHOW THEM YOU'RE BETTER THAN THEY ARE AT SOMETHING THEY LOVE."

—LESLIE KNOPE, *PARKS AND RECREATION*

WHAT, Like IT'S HARD?

It's a real kick in the teeth when your partner one-ups you in the thing toward which you have dedicated hours of your life. What's your first reaction when your partner excels at something that you find challenging or that you thought was yours alone?

You:

_____

_____

_____

_____

_____

_____

_____

Me:

_____

_____

_____

_____

_____

_____

_____

Good FORTUNE!

If you had had your fortunes told when you first met, what would they have said about you?

You:

_____

_____

_____

_____

_____

_____

_____

_____

_____

_____

_____

_____

_____

_____

_____

90

Me:

"I LOVE YOU STRAIGHTFORWARDLY, WITHOUT COMPLEXITIES OR PRIDE; SO I LOVE YOU BECAUSE I KNOW NO OTHER WAY."

—"SONNET XVII: I DO NOT LOVE YOU AS IF YOU WERE," PABLO NERUDA

NAKED Love

Imagine the picture-perfect tribute you might give your partner in a crowd of people or atop the soapbox of social media. Now, cut the nonsense and dress it down to its most natural state. What's the truest way to express your feelings without anyone watching?

You:

_____

_____

_____

_____

_____

_____

Me:

_____

_____

_____

_____

_____

"HELP ME...
I'M FEELING."

—GRINCH, *HOW THE GRINCH STOLE CHRISTMAS*

ALL *the* FEELS!

Sonnets aren't for everybody. If the touchy-feely stuff isn't your bag, you might need more concrete ways to explain why you like kickin' it with your partner. Make a list of the ways your partner makes your world a little less boring, a little less difficult, or even a little...nice!?

You:

_____

_____

_____

_____

_____

_____

Me:

_____

_____

_____

_____

_____

_____

THE LAW of EQUIVALENT VICES

Two video gamers can be together forever, but if one of you is bleary-eyed with a headset at 3 a.m. and the other is wondering why the other side of the bed is still empty, there might be compromise in your future. Which extracurriculars or ways to unwind—be they hobbies, libations, or pints of delicious ice cream—do you see eye to eye on? Where do you need to meet in the middle?

You:

_____

_____

_____

_____

_____

_____

_____

_____

_____

_____

_____

_____

Me:

"WELL, TECHNICALLY
THIS IS YOUR FAULT
BECAUSE WE WERE
AFRAID OUR
MARRIAGE WAS
GETTING AS BORING
AS YOURS."

—CAMERON TUCKER, *MODERN FAMILY*

NOT Too FAR From The TREE

You can try to chuck that apple into another orchard, but chances
are you will be making pie with what you've got. In what ways has
your parents' relationship dynamic taught you what not to do
in your own love life? In what ways would you want to turn into
your parents? (Texting in all caps or inexplicable focus on traffic
patterns not required.)

You:

_____

_____

_____

_____

_____

_____

Me:

_____

_____

_____

_____

_____

_____

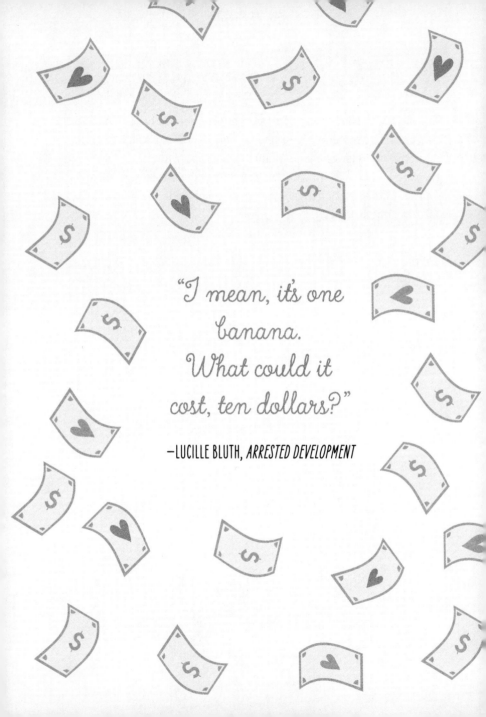

"I mean, it's one banana. What could it cost, ten dollars?"

—LUCILLE BLUTH, *ARRESTED DEVELOPMENT*

MONEY, HONEY

Financial transparency is uncomfortable, but being honest will only make your relationship stronger whether you're in the black or the red. How do you differ in your approach to money and where you choose to spend it? What would help both of you feel less stressed or more empowered about your finances?

You:

_____

_____

_____

_____

_____

_____

Me:

_____

_____

_____

_____

_____

_____

_____

"Without love in the dream,
it will never come true."

—"HELP ON THE WAY," GRATEFUL DEAD

DREAM TEAM!

There is romance in making shit happen. What do you want to do together? What kind of support can you give one another to bring this to fruition?

You:

_____

_____

_____

_____

_____

_____

Me:

_____

_____

_____

_____

_____

_____

OOPSIES

Sometimes you fuck up. Forego the urge of a conditional apology that distances you from accountability. What do you feel sorry about? If things are pretty peachy at the moment, when was a time when you appreciated how your partner apologized?

I'm sorry ~~you feel that way~~.

I'm sorry ~~you thought that~~.

I'm sorry ~~you misinterpreted everything~~.

I'm sorry ~~you overreacted~~.

You:

_____

_____

_____

_____

_____

_____

_____

_____

Pardon!

sorry

Me:

SORRY

"AND I LIKE LARGE PARTIES.
THEY'RE SO INTIMATE.
AT SMALL PARTIES THERE
ISN'T ANY PRIVACY."

—JORDAN BAKER, *THE GREAT GATSBY*

Blink Twice for
GET ME THE FUCK OUT OF HERE

When has the world fallen away and it's just the two of you? Whether it's getting lost in a dark corner or sharing a telepathic moment from across a crowded room because shit is hitting the fan, describe a scenario when you felt totally in sync.

You:

_____

_____

_____

_____

_____

_____

Me:

_____

_____

_____

_____

_____

_____

_____

THIEF of JOY!

When has your lingering frustration about something ruined a perfectly good moment? What could change about a situation like this in the future to shake you out of it and let you enjoy what's in front of you?

You:

_____

_____

_____

_____

_____

_____

Me:

_____

_____

_____

_____

_____

_____

_____

"I can survive just fine without you, you know. But there's a chance that this life can be a little less mundane with you in it."

—SARAH, *PALM SPRINGS*

LIFE is COOL with YOU!

Describe your best adventures together. What things do you normally do that have a way bigger wow-factor as a team? What situations are better with a buddy?

You:

_____

_____

_____

_____

_____

_____

Me:

_____

_____

_____

_____

_____

_____

GREAT *Expectations*

What films, songs, books, or characters defined your earliest expectations of romance? On a scale of 1 to Fucking Nonsense, how closely do they align with your lived experience?

You:

_____

_____

_____

_____

_____

_____

_____

_____

_____

_____

_____

_____

_____

_____

Me:

_____

_____

_____

_____

_____

_____

_____

_____

_____

_____

_____

_____

_____

_____

_____

_____

_____

_____

_____

_____

_____

_____

"I'm in love,
I'M ALIVE,
I belong to the
STARS AND SKY."

—"REAL LOVE BABY," FATHER JOHN MISTY

SHIT'S Getting REAL

Cosmic love has its ups and downs. When has your relationship made you feel completely stellar? When has it felt like there was a fucking asteroid hurtling toward you?

You:

_____

_____

_____

_____

_____

_____

Me:

_____

_____

_____

_____

_____

_____

Bring It Up, BUTTERCUP!

Don't be scared to talk about the serious stuff once in a while, even if it does make one or both of you break out in hives. What big life issues are on your mind that you are worried to bring up? How can you kick ass and take it all on together?

You:

_____

_____

_____

_____

_____

_____

_____

_____

_____

_____

_____

_____

Me:

"Darlin' if you're weary,
Lay your head
upon my chest,
We'll take what
we can carry,
And we'll leave the rest."

—"LAND OF HOPE AND DREAMS," BRUCE SPRINGSTEEN

LET That SH*T GO

Just like that! What have you been holding onto? Is it inconsequential bullshit, literal objects scattered like landmines throughout your home, or is it something important that needs to be spoken out loud?

You:

_____

_____

_____

_____

_____

_____

_____

Me:

_____

_____

_____

_____

_____

_____

_____

"Any day spent with you
IS MY FAVORITE DAY.
So, today is my new
FAVORITE DAY."

—WINNIE-THE-POOH, A. A. MILNE

GOOD DAY to YOU

What do you love best about a routine situation or quick second together in any given day? What flickers of affection do it for you?

You:

_____
_____
_____
_____
_____
_____
_____

Me:

_____
_____
_____
_____
_____
_____
_____

"When something dope comes along, YOU GOTTA LOCK IT DOWN."

—JASON MENDOZA, *THE GOOD PLACE*

GET IT!

The word "relationship" is to commitment-phobes what "moist" is to most of the population. What made *this* relationship sound like fucking poetry to you?

You:

_____

_____

_____

_____

_____

_____

Me:

_____

_____

_____

_____

_____

_____

LOVE is a GIFT!

Welp, that sure sucks for everyone who speaks the other four love languages. Love is what you make it, and being open with how you like to express it and how you hope your partner will give it back is a step toward sharing it more authentically. How do you want to be loved?

You:

_____

_____

_____

_____

_____

_____

_____

_____

_____

_____

_____

_____

Me:

_____

_____

_____

_____

_____

_____

_____

_____

_____

_____

_____

_____

_____

_____

_____

_____

_____

_____

_____

_____

_____

WE are ZEN as F*CK

Hooray! The more open you are with one another, the more at ease you can feel in the great love you share. What about your relationship makes you feel the most tingly with tranquility?

You:

_____

_____

_____

_____

_____

_____

_____

_____

_____

_____

_____

_____

_____

Me:

ABOUT *the* AUTHOR

Monica Sweeney is a writer and editor. Her books include
*Zen as F*ck, Zen as F*ck at Work, Let That Sh*t Go,
Find Your F*cking Happy,* and *You Are My F*cking Sunshine.*
She lives in Boston, Massachusetts.